The Heritage Reformed Congregations
Who We Are and What We Believe

by

Joel R. Beeke

REFORMATION HERITAGE BOOKS
Grand Rapids, Michigan

Published by
Reformation Heritage Books
2965 Leonard St., NE
Grand Rapids, MI 49525
616-977-0599 / Fax 616-285-3246
e-mail: orders@heritagebooks.org
website: www.heritagebooks.org

ISBN #978-1-60178-024-9

For further information on the Heritage Reformed Congregations, write Reformation Heritage Books, 2965 Leonard, N.E., Grand Rapids, Michigan 49525 (616-977-0599, ext. 2), and ask for a free copy of this booklet (additional copies, $2.00 each) and of The HRC Church and School Directory Yearbook *(additional copies, $5.00 each). Additional information can be found at our denominational portal* http://heritagereformed.com *where there are links to various churches' home pages.*

Contents

Introduction

How important is the church to the life of the individual Christian? The sixteenth-century Reformers maintained a high view of the church, while avoiding both the absolutism of Roman Catholicism and the individualism of much of modern American evangelicalism. John Calvin agreed with the early church father Cyprian, who wrote, "He cannot have God for his Father who refuses to have the church for his mother" (*Letters,* iv. 4). To this Calvin added, "For there is no other way to enter into life unless this mother conceive us in her womb, give us birth, nourish us at her breast, and lastly, unless she keep us under her care and guidance until, putting off mortal flesh, we become like the angels" (*Institutes,* 4.1.4).

In the past, Reformed believers profoundly cherished the church. Today, that sense of appreciation is waning in general; many Protestants have depreciated the place the church occupies as Christ's institution. This lower view of the church is fostered by a lack of understanding about what the church truly is as Christ's institution. It disregards Jesus' words to Peter, "Upon this rock I will build my church" (Matt. 16:18). These words address the status of the church as belonging to Christ ("My church"), the substance of the church as founded upon Christ ("upon this rock"), and the success of the church as the workmanship of Christ ("I will build")—all of which should increasingly prompt us to cherish the church.

Cherishing the church as the universal bride of Christ in her invisible form goes hand in hand with valuing and being committed to the church's visible manifestation in terms of specific churches and denominations. Too often today, church members do not understand their own church and denomination, with the result that they do not love it enough. Then, too, denominations often do a poor job of communicating their beliefs, distinctives, and ministries to those who may be interested in knowing them, especially similar-minded churches around them. This booklet seeks to address this need for the relatively new Heritage Reformed Congregations by setting forth its goal and vision; origin and history; doctrinal standards and worship; biblical, doctrinal, experiential, practical, and ecclesiastical emphases; and its denominational ministries. Our prayer is that this booklet will promote a deeper appreciation of and commitment to Christ's bride, as laid out in Scripture and envisioned by the Reformers, as she functions within the Heritage Reformed denomination.

Chapter 1

Goal and Vision, Origin and History

The Heritage Reformed Congregations (hereafter, HRC) is a solidly biblical, Reformed, and orthodox denomination that is confessionally rooted in the Continental Reformation and influenced greatly by English Puritanism. The word "Heritage" in the title reflects a commitment and desire to be true to this rich legacy.

Goal and Vision

Despite many shortcomings, Heritage Reformed churches are earnest about believing Reformed doctrine with our minds, experiencing Reformed truth in our hearts, and living the Reformed faith throughout our lives. By the Spirit's grace, the primary goal of the HRC is prayerfully and actively to communicate our Reformed heritage among our churches and throughout the world in biblically meaningful ways, discipling believers and evangelizing unbelievers for the worship and glory of God by means of local churches, seminaries, and evangelism and missions. To fulfill this goal, we strive through the Spirit to use biblically principled and sanctioned means to assist us in carrying out the vision of being:

- Word-based and Christ-centered churches,
- Sacramental and disciplined churches,
- Confessing and worshiping churches,
- Learning and growing churches,
- Praying and working churches,
- Loving and sacrificial churches,
- Discipling and evangelizing churches,
- Servant-led and equipping churches,
- Sanctified and separated churches,
- Humble and penitent churches,
- Sin-hating and conscience-sensitized churches,
- Believing and praising churches.

In short, we strive to be churches that glorify God as commanded in His Word.

Origin and History

The Heritage Reformed denomination was established in 1993 after the Netherlands Reformed Congregations (hereafter, NRC) underwent a split related to church-orderly and theological issues. The most substantive underlying issue to future HRC members and congregations was Christ-centered preaching, combined with the preaching of an unconditional offer of grace. In the first few years, churches were established in Grand Rapids, Michigan; Woodstock (now Burgessville), Ontario; St. Catharines (now Jordan), Ontario; Hull, Iowa; Bradford, Ontario; Fort Macleod, Alberta; Pompton Plains (now Franklin Lakes), New Jersey; and Plymouth, Wisconsin.

Presently, the HRC consists of approximately two thousand members in North American churches from the East Coast (New Jersey) to the West Coast (British Columbia). Most of her ministers labor in North America, though three are presently laboring in Africa—two in South Africa and one in Zambia.

Chapter 2

Doctrinal Standards and Worship

Heritage Reformed congregations, office-bearers, and members affirm the three Ecumenical Creeds (Apostles', Nicene, and Athanasian) and the three Reformed Forms of Unity as biblically sound doctrinal standards:

- The Belgic Confession of Faith (1561; written primarily by Guido DeBrès),
- The Heidelberg Catechism (1563; written primarily by Zacharias Ursinus and Caspar Olevianus), and
- The Canons of Dort (1618-19; written by the Reformed Synod convened at Dordrecht, the Netherlands). (To purchase a copy of these Doctrinal Standards, write orders@heritagebooks.org.)

Though not yet officially adopted, the HRC also concurs with the Westminster Standards of the 1640s: the Westminster Confession of Faith, and the Larger and Shorter Catechisms.

Most congregations periodically read the Belgic Confession and the Canons of Dort at worship services, and offer weekly preaching based on the Heidelberg Catechism except on special occasions, such as church feast days or on a Communion Sabbath. The ministers follow an ecclesiastical calendar, which includes preaching messages that relate to the great redemptive-historical acts of salvation, from Advent to Pentecost, while the congregants are admonished to avoid all commercialization of these "feast days." For the majority of their sermons, however, most ministers proclaim God's Word in an expository fashion, preaching their way through various Bible books or sections of Scripture.

The HRC places a premium on expository preaching because it explains and applies a particular portion of God's Word in its context. A commitment to expositional preaching is important because it gives authority to the preacher since he is bringing *God's* Word and because such preaching is best suited to moving a church to hear and obey God's Word.

Our English word *worship* is derived from the word *worth*. Worship is really "worthship" and reminds us that God is worthy of receiving our praise and honor. Consequently, godly sobriety dominates worship in the HRC out of deep reverence for God and His holy congregation. We see ourselves as guests in His house, praying that we will worship and exalt Him in a pure, unalloyed manner, supremely for His glory, and will remember that true worship is what God enjoys and commands and has a right to expect. Our worship must be corporate, Christ-exalting, and celebrative; above all else, it must be thoroughly biblical. This "regulative principle of worship," requiring that every part of worship must be grounded in Scripture, is assiduously adhered to as the only principle that can withstand today's sweeping tide of unbiblical, shallow, worldly, informal, and innovative human worship. Everything in divine worship must be warranted by Scripture. We believe that in worship we enter into a dialogue with God whereby we humbly bring our adoration, confession, thanksgiving, and supplications to Him. We do that through prayers, congregational singing of the Psalms, offerings, and benedictions, which take up approximately half of a typical worship service. The other half of our service is devoted to the reading of Scripture and preaching the whole counsel of God's Word—both law and gospel, both death in Adam and life in Christ, both divine sovereignty and human responsibility. Through the reading and preaching of His Word, God speaks to us, instructing, strengthening, equipping, chastising, and warning us for our good. We strive to ensure that all the biblical aspects of worship are included in our services: proclamation and learning of truth, adoration, repentance, intercession, dedication and thanksgiving.

We believe that it is critical for the preacher to conduct the service with the consciousness that he is in the presence of Almighty God. All self- or man-centeredness, casual demeanor, chatty and superfluous comments must be avoided in public worship when in the presence of the King of kings. Reflective of the church's calling, preaching must be biblical, doctrinal, experiential, and practical. Let us now take a closer look at these four emphases, then consider the HRC's ecclesiastical emphases and denominational ministries.

Chapter 3

Biblical Emphasis:
Church, Home, and School

The HRC wholeheartedly affirms the divine inspiration, sufficiency, clarity, authority, and necessity of Scripture. Such is Scripture's self-attestation (2 Tim. 3:16; 2 Pet. 1:20-21; Heb. 1:1-2, 4:12). We believe that this supernatural divine inspiration ceased with the closing of the canon, so that Scripture alone remains the living voice of God to the church today.

At church, home, and school, we covet the power of the Spirit that makes sinners wise unto salvation through the Scriptures.

Church
The Authorized (often called, "King James") Version of the Bible is used in HRC worship services, being judged a faithful translation of the authentic and preserved texts. We also wish to avoid the confusion that arises from the use of a variety of translations in church services. All ministers stress scriptural exposition in their preaching, teaching, and pastoral visitation. Local church meetings are immersed in the Scriptures; meetings of the combined churches, called classes (singular: classis), strive to do everything in accord with the Scriptures. All instruction given in various teaching situations aims to ground itself in the Scriptures.

Home
The HRC encourages and admonishes its members to be intensely Word-centered in faith and practice. We believe that as we learn to think, speak, and act more biblically, our teaching will become more effective and our witness more fruitful. This belief is particularly dear with regard to the children of the congregations in our covenant homes. Great care is taken to educate the children in the Bible from an early age not only in church or at Christian schools, but also at home. The family altar is a place of daily prayer, reading and discussion of Scripture, and songs of praise.

School
Christian education that centers on the Scripture receives a high priority in the

HRC, often at great personal sacrifice for parents. Most of the denomination's children attend schools that strive to educate children in sound, biblical teaching from pre-K through Grade 12.

In sum, the HRC sets a high premium on reading, searching, meditating, knowing, believing, singing, loving, praying, living, and practicing the Scriptures. Our prayer is that God would enable us increasingly to become Word-centered.

Chapter 4

Doctrinal Emphasis: Major Teachings

Preaching and worship services stress the vertical line of the gospel; a right relationship with God is indispensable for God-glorifying relationships with others.

Consequently, the focus of most preaching in the HRC is the Triune God, together with our need to be saved in and through His Son. Jesus Christ is the center and heartbeat of every message. God's being, names, attributes, divine Persons, and work—the electing love of the Father, the redeeming love of the Son, and the applying love of the Holy Spirit—are emphasized. Preaching underscores the biblical balance between God's justice and His love; divine love is preached without the relinquishment of divine justice. The Lord is too holy and righteous to forgive sin through any means other than the substitutionary sufferings and death of His only-begotten Son.

Christ and His salvation are freely offered to all sinners without exception. By the Spirit's grace, this gospel offer is the warrant for all sinners to receive and rely on Christ alone for salvation. Whoever truly repents of sin, and believes in and looks to Christ alone for salvation receives the forgiveness of sin and a title to eternal life in the blessedness of heaven.

Doctrinally, the HRC is thoroughly Protestant and Reformed. All significant doctrines of the Scriptures that fall under the six major divisions of Protestant theology are proclaimed in an unequivocally Reformed manner. These include:

- Theology proper: doctrines about God, such as His being, names, attributes, triune character, and decrees;
- Anthropology: doctrines about man, such as our creation, our bearing of God's image, the covenant of works, our fall in Adam, and our sin and punishment;
- Christology: doctrines about Christ, such as His names, offices, natures, states, and benefits, as well as the covenant of grace;
- Soteriology: doctrines about salvation, such as effectual calling, regeneration, conversion, repentance, faith, justification, adoption, sanctification, assurance, and perseverance;

- Ecclesiology: doctrines about the church, such as its essence and marks, and the means of grace—especially preaching and the sacraments;

- Eschatology: doctrines about the last things, such as death, the intermediate state, immortality of the soul, the second coming of Christ, the resurrection, final judgment, heaven, and hell. (For a doctrinal summary of these areas of doctrine, see Appendix 1; for a personal summary, see Appendix 2.)

The churches also promote the five Reformation watchwords or battle cries, centered around the Latin word *solus,* meaning "alone," that is, "only." These watchwords capsulate Protestant teaching in contrast to Roman Catholicism in the following ways:

Protestant	Roman Catholic
Scripture alone *(sola Scriptura)*	Scripture and tradition
Faith alone *(sola fide)*	Faith and works
Grace alone *(sola gratia)*	Grace and merits
Christ alone *(solus Christus)*	Christ, Mary, and intercession of saints
Glory to God alone *(soli Deo gloria)*	God, saints, and church hierarchy

Briefly, this is what these five watchwords mean for us today:

- *Scripture only:* The Bible is the inspired, infallible, and inerrant Word of God, and it is the *only* rule and authority for faith and practice. This means that we endeavor to submit unconditionally to everything the Bible teaches (2 Tim. 3:16).

- *Grace only:* We can *only* be saved from sin and its consequences by the renewing work of the Holy Spirit. This manifestation of God's sovereign goodness to sinners, which excludes all human merit, the Bible calls the grace of God (Eph. 2:8). Our salvation is altogether of God; from beginning to end, it is *only* by God's free mercy and grace.

- *Faith only:* Salvation is not the result of our own accomplishments or works, but is obtained *only* by faith in the Lord Jesus Christ and His atonement accomplished on Calvary's cross. By faith in the perfect obedience of Christ we become righteous before God, trusting *only* in the finished work of Christ (Heb. 4:2).

- *Christ only:* The Lord Jesus Christ is the *only* Mediator between God and man (1 Tim. 2:5), who has made an effective, complete, and final atonement for sin. Therefore He is the *only* One through whom we can be reconciled with our Creator, whom we have offended by our sins. *Only* Christ's perfect sacrifice and righteousness are acceptable to God (John 14:6), and through Him we have direct access to God.

- *Glory to God only:* The primary purpose of our existence is to live to God's glory, which therefore is the primary purpose of our salvation. This means that all honor and glory for our salvation must be given to God *only* (Rev. 7:12).

The HRC stresses the sovereignty of God's grace in salvation, which is powerfully illustrated by the so-called "Five Points of Calvinism" as formulated by the Synod of Dort, now commonly known by their acronym, TULIP. These five points can be succinctly summarized as follows:

- *Total depravity* (sovereign grace needed): man is so depraved and corrupted by sin in every part of his being that he is by nature incapable of doing any spiritual good and cannot effect any part of his salvation (Gen. 6:5);

- *Unconditional election* (sovereign grace conceived): from eternity past, God chose to save certain individuals irrevocably to everlasting life and glory in Christ Jesus without seeing any intrinsic goodness in them, and He ordained the means by which they would be saved (Rom. 9:15-16);

- *Limited atonement* (sovereign grace merited): while the death of Christ is sufficient to cover the sins of the world, its saving efficacy is intentionally limited to His elect sheep whose sins He bore and for whom He fully satisfied the justice of God (John 17:9);

- *Irresistible grace* (sovereign grace applied): God irresistibly calls the elect to saving faith and salvation in Christ with such sovereign power that they can no longer resist His grace, but are made willing in the day of His power (Ps. 110:3; John 6:44-45); and,

- *Perseverance* (sovereign grace preserved): those whom God saves, He graciously preserves in the state of grace so that they will never be lost. They may be troubled by infirmities as they seek to make their calling and election sure, but they will persevere until the end, fighting the good fight of faith until the final victory shall be realized in the coming again of their Savior and Lord as Judge (John 10:28).

Though the five *solas* summarize major dimensions of doctrinal Calvinism and the five points summarize soteriological Calvinism, these ten teachings do not summarize all of Calvinism. That would leave us with a truncated view of the Reformed faith. To mention only a few additional areas, we believe that Calvinism also involves:

- A Reformed view of worship in general and the sacraments in particular,

- A comprehensive embracing of the lordship of Christ over every sphere of life,
- A biblical view of marriage and family,
- A providential conviction about one's vocation,
- A strong impetus to evangelism and piety,
- A biblical and realistic view of the covenant and of covenant children,
- In most cases, a Presbyterian or Reformed form of church government.

In short, the Reformed faith is passionately committed to bring every thought and area of life into captivity to the service of Christ.

We believe that all these doctrines of grace give glory to God, are pastorally encouraging, strengthen believers, and earnestly and lovingly call unbelievers to come to Christ without delay.

Chapter 5

Experiential Emphasis: Applicatory and Discriminatory Preaching

Experiential or experimental preaching addresses how a Christian experiences the truth of Christian doctrine in his life. The term *experimental* comes from the Latin *experimentum,* meaning "trial." It is derived from the verb *experior,* meaning "to try, prove, or put to the test." That same verb can also mean "to find or know by experience," thus leading to the word *experiential,* meaning knowledge gained by experiment. John Calvin used *experiential* and *experimental* interchangeably, since both words in biblical preaching indicate the need for measuring experienced knowledge against the touchstone of Scripture.

By experiential or experimental preaching, we mean Christ-centered preaching which stresses that for salvation sinners must by faith have a personal, experiential (that is, experienced) Spirit-worked knowledge of Christ, and, by extension, of all the great truths of Scripture. Thus the HRC emphasizes, as the Puritans did, that the Holy Spirit causes the objective truths about Christ and His work to be experienced in the heart and life of sinners.

For example, our lost state and condition by nature due to our tragic fall in Adam, our dire need for Jesus Christ who merits and applies salvation by His Spirit, and our responsibility to repent and believe the gospel of God's freely offered salvation in Jesus Christ all must be known and experienced in our lives. The HRC stresses that the Holy Spirit blesses man-abasing, Christ-centered preaching that makes room for Christ within the soul; believers will then yearn to live wholly for His glory out of gratitude for His great salvation. John 17:3 says, "And this is life eternal, that they might know thee the only true God, and Jesus Christ, whom thou hast sent." The gospel truth of sovereign grace that abases us to the lowest and exalts Christ to the highest in our salvation must be proclaimed and experienced.

Experiential preaching is therefore *applicatory.* It explains how matters do go (Rom. 7:14-25) and how they ought to go in the Christian life (Rom. 8). It explains how the life of faith begins with spiritual rebirth and grows in resisting sin and in becoming Christ-like while being indwelt by the Holy Spirit. It aims to apply faith in Christ to all of the believer's experience as an individual and in all the believer's relationships in the family, church, and world. Such preaching addresses the mind, engages the heart, and confronts the conscience.

Experiential preaching is also *discriminatory*. It defines the difference between believers and unbelievers, opening the kingdom of heaven to believers and shutting it against unbelievers. HRC members believe that more than historical faith (believing biblical truth and doctrine with the mind) is necessary for salvation. True saving faith (biblical doctrine and truth formed within the soul by personal knowledge of and trust in Christ alone for salvation) is essential. At minimum a true Christian should be able to explain the basics of personal conversion, which results in experiencing the reality of the guilt of sin, deliverance in Christ, and gratitude to the Triune God for His glorious salvation.

Emphasis must be placed, then, on the necessity of being born again, repenting, and believing in Christ alone for salvation. True conversion should never be presumed in adults or children. The child growing up in the church receives the outward benefits of the covenant, but the covenant's essence and promises must be appropriated by faith and repentance. We are opposed to an overly optimistic view of the covenant that regards covenant children as in a state of grace unless the opposite proves true later in life. Out of loving concern for children and adults, biblical marks and fruits of saving grace are expounded from Scripture to distinguish spiritual life from counterfeit Christianity.

Reformed experiential preaching teaches that Christianity is not only a creed and a way of life but also an inner experience resulting from personal fellowship with God through the indwelling Spirit. Some assert that this produces an unbiblical kind of mysticism, but nothing could be further from the truth. Unbiblical mysticism separates Christian experience from the Word of God, but the historic Reformed stance demands God-glorifying, Word-centered, Spirit-worked experiential Christianity. Such Christianity produces a balanced Calvinism that does justice to all aspects of the Christian life: the intellectual, the emotional, the volitional, and the spiritual. It helps promote a comprehensive Reformed worldview. It shows us how to live in two worlds; how to have heaven before our minds to guide and shape our lives here on earth. (For a more detailed explanation of experiential preaching, order the booklet, *The Lasting Power of Reformed Experiential Preaching,* from orders@ heritagebooks.org.)

Chapter 6

Practical Emphasis:
Holiness and Commitment

Since God has a right to call and command His church to be holy in Christ, a church that is unholy in practice is an oxymoron. The HRC not only endeavors to buttress the historic Reformed position biblically, doctrinally, and experientially, but also practically in daily life. By the Spirit's grace, it fosters holiness and spiritual growth through opportunities of worship, learning, fellowship, witness, and service. Three such areas warrant further attention.

Called to Comprehensive Holiness

God calls believers to be holy as He is holy (1 Pet. 1:16). God's holiness testifies of His purity, His moral perfection, His separateness from all outside of Him, and His complete absence of sin (Job 34:10; Isa. 5:16; 40:18; Hab. 1:13). For us, holiness means, negatively, to be separate from sin and, positively, to be consecrated to God and conformed to Christ. We believe, then, that holiness of mind and heart and life must be cultivated in every sphere of life: in privacy with God, in the confidentiality of our homes, in the competitiveness of our occupation, in the pleasures of social friendships, in our interactions with unevangelized neighbors and the world's hungry and unemployed, as well as in Sunday worship. In short, holiness inwardly must fill our entire heart and outwardly must cover all of life (1 Thess. 5:23).

No one can acquire holiness by his own efforts. Nevertheless, believers are granted holiness in their status with God the moment they trust in Christ alone for salvation. Our holy standing with God in Christ, however, does not imply that we have arrived at a wholly sanctified condition (1 Cor. 1:2). That is why the New Testament presents holiness as something believers have in Christ and something they must still cultivate in the strength of Christ. As believers, our status in holiness is conferred, but our condition in holiness must be pursued. Thus, in Christian living, we are called to be in life what we already are in principle by grace, in dependence on the Spirit. Cultivating holiness means imitating the character of the Father, conforming to the image of Christ, and submitting to the mind of the Spirit. To that end, we must use the means of grace (including diligent Bible study, worshipful church attendance, joyous Sabbath-keeping, deepening prayer and earnest prayer meetings, vibrant family worship, habitual meditation, loving fellowship, heartfelt singing, disciplined witnessing, faithful service, and principled stewardship), all the while reckoning ourselves as dead to the dominion of sin and as alive to God in Christ (Rom. 6:11).

Called to Commitment in the World

The HRC believes that this call to holiness is not separate from our call of commitment to disciple believers and to evangelize the world (Matt. 28:18-20). Just as Abram became involved in the affairs of this world by collecting his 318 servants to pursue enemy kings and recapture Lot (Gen. 14), so believers today must fight the good fight of faith and be committed to the world's welfare in a positive, creative, and helpful way. Genuine piety doesn't escape from the world but seeks to influence the world for good.

The HRC believes our commitment to this world involves being concerned about God's reputation, the souls of believers around us, and the lost state of millions in our world today. We are called to disciple fellow believers around us by fellowshipping with them, allowing "iron to sharpen iron," and by encouraging and exhorting each other to immerse ourselves in the Word of God, diligently to use the means of grace, and daily to walk in "the King's highway of holiness" by keeping all His commandments. Moreover, we are called to reach out to the unsaved and to commit to bringing them the gospel urgently and earnestly in a variety of ways, calling sinners to repent and believe on Christ. We must use our time, resources, and gifts to lead people to a saving faith in Christ, a deeper fellowship and fruitful service. We need to be committed to the world, remembering that the church that doesn't evangelize will fossilize. At the same time, we must remain independent and separated from the world, remembering that we must not be compromised by its way of thinking, speaking, and acting.

Called to Separation from Worldliness

The HRC denomination takes God's Word seriously when the Lord commands His people not to mingle with worldly people, worldly customs, worldly practices, and worldly places. Not to merit salvation but as an inevitable consequence of salvation, the believer will "come out from the world and be separate" as God's Word commands (2 Cor. 6:17). Therefore, the church must speak out against that which provokes "the lust of the flesh, and the lust of the eyes, and the pride of life" (1 John 2:16). Church members are admonished to avoid immodest dress, idolization of sports or movie heroes, ungodly lyrics and music, addictions such as alcoholism and gluttony, materialism, and an uncontrolled use of any modern media that glamorize sin. Scripture plainly states: "Abstain from all appearance of evil" (1 Thess. 5:22).

This biblically conservative way of life, far from being meritorious, is a spontaneous outgrowth of bowing gratefully under divine Lordship. The true Christian should war against every desire that would set his heart on sinful trivialities of this world that tend to interrupt his close walk with God.

The Christian's life is meant to be a preparation for the life to come. His godly walk and tempered concern over the lawful matters of this world will cause him to be the salt of the earth and the light on the hill. His walk, his talk, and even his withdrawal and silence should testify to the living principle of real Christianity within him.

The HRC warns against two extremes in spirituality today: worldliness and "otherworldliness." On the one hand, it rejects the line of thought that *literally* separates its members from the world. We maintain the biblical injunction that Christians must remain *in* but not *of* the world. On the other hand, the denomination also rejects the notion that the Christian is so otherworldly that he can sanctify worldly transactions and happenings merely by his or her presence and intervention. We fear that this approach only provides a license to sin and usually ends in lukewarmness and worldliness. It strips the body of Christ of its precious heritage as an antithesis to the world. Instead, in a post-Christian culture, we must strive to be a positive and holy counterforce to the swelling tide of secularism.

Chapter 7

Ecclesiastical Emphasis

The HRC believes that a true church is recognized by faithful preaching of the Word of God, faithful and proper administration of the sacraments, and faithful exercise of biblical discipline (Phil. 2:16; Acts 20:7; Matt. 18:15-17).

Church Mixture

The HRC believes that the local church should be viewed as it is in reality, namely, a covenant congregation of the Lord consisting of a mixed group of people. This mixture includes strong and weak believers, unbelievers and hypocrites, wheat and chaff. Preaching should reflect this reality by taking into account the various spiritual conditions of the members of the congregation and appropriately addressing them. The preacher must constantly set the promises and demands of the Word before church members, reminding them that they must be radically renewed and grow in accord with those promises and demands through the Holy Spirit. The church needs to continually know the presence, ministry, and blessing of the Holy Spirit for sanctification, fellowship, worship, evangelism, and government. The real strength of a church does not lie in its size and wealth but in the spiritual renewal, growth, and vitality of its members.

Church Intercession

We believe that a healthy church is an intercessory church. The HRC stresses prayer from the pulpit, in private, and in gathered meetings. Most churches have regular, formal prayer meetings as well as informal, smaller group prayer meetings in various homes.

We believe that intercessory prayer meetings are important to:

- Glorify and worship God together in the most intimate way possible,
- Employ the spiritual life of the church for the good of all the church's ministries,
- Increase the Christ-centeredness and diminish the self-centeredness of believers,
- Unite believers together at God's throne of grace,

- Use the spiritual life of the church for the good of all the church's ministries,
- Exercise mutual sympathy among the members,
- Encourage each other to holiness,
- Edify each other through the communication of each other's gifts,
- Assist mutual accountability and counseling of each other,
- Initiate or increase revival, by God's grace,
- Augment commitment to Christ's kingdom in evangelistic and mission work, at home, and abroad,
- Provide a spiritual oasis of fellowship in the midst of a busy week in the world,
- Promote respect and appreciation for each other, and
- Demonstrate complete dependence on God for His indispensable blessing upon His ministries in the church.

Church Government

The HRC adheres to a Reformed form of church government in which each congregation is governed by a consistory consisting of minister(s), elders, and deacons. Twice each year, HRC churches meet together at its broadest assembly, called classis. At this meeting, the churches' delegates discuss reports from various committees, consider and debate various points submitted by the churches, hear reports on the spiritual well-being of each congregation, and provide mutual advice, support, and encouragement. Decisions made by classis are considered binding unless they can be shown to be in conflict with the Word of God. The 1914 redaction of the Church Order of Dort (a revision of the original 1618-19 Church Order) is used to guide the churches in their decision-making at both a classical and consistorial level.

Church Membership

The HRC believes that church membership is a biblical directive and is essential to the true life and proper functioning of the church and the enjoyment of its fellowship (Matt. 18:17; Eph. 2:20-22, 4:11-12; Col. 2:5). Church membership is taken seriously by the HRC. Most churches ask prospective members to attend a "confession of faith" class for a year (usually taught by a minister) before committing to full membership.

Professing members receive numerous rights and responsibilities. Rights include the use of the sacraments, the guidance and prayers of the consistory as well as the opportunity to bring to them one's personal convictions, family visitation by the church officers, pastoral visitation in illness, and the loving discipline of the elders and the practical assistance of the deacons, when needed. Rights also include the love and care of fellow members shown in fellowshipping and forgiving and forbearing each other, the opportunity to use gifts and talents in a variety of church ministries, and the participation in and voting at congregational meetings for male members. Responsibilities include supporting the congregation by maintaining biblical truth, attending church faithfully, respecting and praying for the leaders and members and ministries of the church, and cultivating brotherly unity and love toward other members. Responsibilities also include promoting mutual peace and biblical counsel, living a Word-centered and godly life that flees worldliness, inviting the unchurched to attend and warmly welcoming those who visit, seeking to use God-given gifts in church ministry, developing an attitude of servanthood, and exercising biblical stewardship in giving financially to church ministries.

Church Sacraments

The HRC administers two sacraments: Holy Baptism and the Lord's Supper. Baptism is given to all professing members and their children. The Lord's Supper is administered four to six times a year for professing members in good standing who confess their sin and misery, hope in Christ alone for salvation, and yearn to live a life of gratitude and holiness before God. Since only those who are able to examine themselves maturely are allowed to partake of the Lord's Supper (1 Cor. 11:28), we reject inviting children to the Table.

Church Fellowship

The HRC seeks to enter into correspondence and fellowship with other churches and denominations who embrace similar convictions. Presently, the denomination is in correspondence and fellowship with the Free Reformed Churches of North America and the Free Church of Scotland (Continuing). Dialogue with churches in Australia, South Africa, and the Netherlands is also ongoing.

Church Error

We cannot deny that serious error abounds on every hand in the worldwide church and the world. The HRC believes that we have a polemical task to speak out against unbelief, false teaching, and the sins of the times. We must defend the faith once delivered to the saints (Jude 3) and refuse to conform to worldly standards of political correctness. We must oppose all liberalism, ritualism, humanism, and post-modern theology that abound in our culture.

We must oppose all new doctrines such as the New Perspective on Paul and Federal Vision (which promotes hyper-covenantalism) that wage war against the truths of Scripture. We must oppose old but popular errors such as the Charismatic movement because it undermines the absolute sufficiency of Scripture, claims extra-biblical revelation through miraculous gifts, and teaches an unscriptural post-conversion experience that belittles the great work of regeneration. We must stand on the Lord's side on issues related to women bearing office in the church, homosexuality in the church, and various forms of evolutionary theory, such as theistic evolution, day-age theory, and the framework hypothesis. We also condemn all errors that militate against God as the divine Being of comprehensive providence, such as pantheism, deism, and open theism (Acts 14:14-18; 17:24-28; Heb. 1:3). We also oppose sins that abound on every hand in our post-modern society, such as homosexual marriage, terrorism, Sabbath-desecration, abortion, immorality, blasphemy, and the rejection of authority. We must be biblical and contemporary in combating error.

Chapter 8

Denominational Ministries

In obedience to Christ's commission to be a teaching, learning, praying, working, loving, and evangelistic church, the HRC is involved in a number of denominational and local ministries. They include:

Puritan Reformed Theological Seminary

Owned and governed by the HRC, the Puritan Reformed Theological Seminary (established in 1995; hereafter, PRTS) prepares students to serve Christ and His church through biblical, experiential, and practical ministry. PRTS students come from numerous Reformed and Presbyterian denominations as well as independent Baptist churches. They hail from various countries, such as Australia, Brazil, Canada, China, England, Indonesia, Korea, Nigeria, and South Africa.

PRTS offers three programs: a Master of Arts in Religion (a two-year degree, which usually serves as a transitional degree to doctoral work), a Master of Divinity degree (a four-year ministerial degree), and a Master of Theology degree (a degree that involves a year or more of advanced study beyond the ministerial degree and is often taken by students who desire to teach in seminaries around the world). The training in each program is rigorous and thoroughly Reformed. All of the programs are fully licensed by the State of Michigan and aim to be of the highest caliber. PRTS is accredited by the Association of Reformed Theological Seminaries (ARTS) and has obtained federal permission to enroll students from foreign countries.

Presently, PRTS serves about sixty students and is staffed with three full-time professors (Dr. Joel Beeke, President and Professor of Systematic Theology, Homiletics, and Church History; Dr. Gerald Bilkes, Professor of Old and New Testament; and Dr. David Murray, Professor of Old Testament and Practical Theology) and thirty-five part-time professors (including Dr. Sinclair Ferguson, Dr. James Grier, Dr. Michael Haykin, Dr. Hywel Jones, Dr. David Lachman, Rev. Ray Lanning, Dr. Richard Muller, Dr. Robert Oliver, Rev. Neil Pronk, Rev. Maurice Roberts, Dr. Derek Thomas, and Rev. Geoff Thomas).

PRTS houses a 45,000-volume library that includes the Puritan Resource Center, a collection of more than 3,000 volumes by and about the Puritans in a separate climate-controlled room. The center's special treasure is a collection of hundreds of antiquarian volumes, many of them rare items with only a few copies known to exist in the world. The center was created to foster study of the Puritans by ministers, seminary professors, and theological students throughout the world.

For a catalog and DVD of the seminary programs, or to receive a quarterly *PRTS Update* and be placed on the seminary's mailing list, contact PRTS at 2965 Leonard N.E., Grand Rapids, Michigan 49525; or Mr. Henk Kleyn at 616-977-0599, ext. 120; henk.kleyn@puritanseminary.org. You may also visit the PRTS website at www.puritanseminary.org.

Elementary and Secondary Christian Education
Most HRC parents make great sacrifices to send their children to our own Christian schools or schools jointly operated with the NRC. Some make use of other Christian schools or undertake home schooling. Few send their children to public schools.

The primary reason for this commitment is that raising covenant children is a solemn responsibility. Parents are duty bound to educate their children in an atmosphere that reflects their biblical convictions about truth, spiritual life, and parenting. Because the world's presuppositions and philosophy of education are antithetical to the teachings of the church, most HRC parents believe that covenant children should not be educated in a curriculum that is hostile to what they are striving to teach their children at home and at church.

HRC parents do not look for a Christian school that only attaches the Bible to its curriculum and removes the children from an overtly worldly setting. Rather, they seek to educate children in a curriculum that is decidedly Christ-centered and Reformed in its presuppositions, its philosophical outlook, its theological content, and its practical outworkings. They look for a school that puts God, man, facts, the universe, existence, origins, purpose, morality, history, aspirations, and absolutes in their proper, biblical, God-defined contexts.

Missions
The Heritage Reformed Congregations, in obedience to Christ's great commission to His church, is actively engaged in the propagation of the gospel both at home and abroad. To carry out this sacred obligation, the Mission Committee's formal statement of purpose is as follows:

> The purpose of the HRC missions program is to glorify God and present His character and nature by effectively proclaiming the message of salvation in Jesus Christ throughout the world, in order that lost

sinners might be brought to salvation through the blood of Christ (from the HRC Mission Handbook).

The Mission Committee has established the following organizational structure:

At present, the primary thrust of the denomination's foreign mission efforts is to focus on assisting and nurturing young Christian churches in developing countries by providing and improving training for pastors. The HRC sponsors three full-time missionary pastors.

Dr. Arthur Miskin and family are laboring in South Africa where Rev. Miskin is teaching at Mukhanyo Theological College. Rev. Miskin and his wife, Dr. Sonja Miskin, are also utilizing their skills as medical doctors to assist AIDS victims and orphans of AIDS victims via the Masibambisane Community Development Corporation, a nearby humanitarian relief organization.

Rev. Brian DeVries, who is just completing his Ph.D. in missions, is being sent out this summer (2007) to work with Dr. Miskin and teach at Mukhanyo Theological College. Rev. and Mrs. Cees Molenaar and their family are serving the Lord as a missionary family in Zambia. Rev. Molenaar serves as principal at Covenant College, a theological seminary that is supported in part by the Free Church of Scotland (Continuing).

Individuals in the HRC give considerable support to independent mission workers laboring in a variety of places, including Mexico, Cambodia, Nigeria, and Indonesia. Prayer is offered regularly that God will send more missionaries and mission workers into the harvest. The need is great (John 4:35; Matt. 9:37-38).

Evangelism and Church Planting
The HRC is engaged in numerous evangelistic and church-planting efforts. Our churches continue to take seriously their calling to spread the gospel, beginning locally. In most congregations, local evangelism committees are zealous in bringing the gospel to the lost in a variety of ways. Current methods

include Bible studies, radio ministry, neighborhood Sunday school, Vacation Bible School, tract distribution, nursing home outreach, ministries for the homeless, and jail or prison ministry. Local churches are also encouraged to consider church plants in their own geographical area.

Radio, Tape/CD, Internet, Audio, and Other Forms of Outreach

The HRC is active in radio outreach as a denomination in several cities and, in some cases, in local church areas. Radio programs are aired on a weekly basis, the most effective being in New York City.

"The Tape Room," which includes sermons of most HRC ministers, maintains an extensive tape ministry throughout North America. Numerous tapes and CDs are purchased and loaned each year. For a catalog of available tapes, write "The Tape Room," 540 Crescent, N.E., Grand Rapids, Michigan 49503. Thousands of HRC sermons are also downloaded around the world each month from www.sermonaudio.com, on which several churches post their ministers' sermons each week. Also, some churches offer live (real time) audio and video streaming of church sermons.

A wide variety of material can be downloaded from our denominational Web portal, www.heritagereformed.com. Some local churches also have their own Web page with archived sermons and are linked to this main website. A few HRC ministers write books and articles for various periodicals, speak at conferences in United States and abroad, and lecture at various seminaries.

The HRC offers youth camps, men's conferences, women's conferences, and family conferences on an annual or biennial basis. Youth groups and women's groups reach out in a number of ways to the poor and needy in local communities. Various local church choirs are active in reaching their communities with God-glorifying music. Several churches are very active in jail and prison ministries.

Publications

HRC members promote sound Reformed literature around the world, including:

- The *Banner of Sovereign Grace Truth,* the official family periodical of the denomination, which is published ten times per year (bsgt@hnrc.org);
- Banner of Truth Tract Mission, which distributes tens of thousands of tracts around the world each year and thousands of sermons to prisoners in various U.S. jails (bsgt@hnrc.org);
- *Glad Tidings,* the official mission publication of the denomination (JaneKorevaar@sympatico.ca);

- Gospel Trumpet sermons, written by HRC ministers and printed three sermons per booklet, distributed free of charge;

- Inheritance Publishers (IP), which publishes approximately four out-of-print pocket sermons per year (23,000 booklets per printing) of Reformed ministers from the 16th-19th centuries, and distributes them free of charge around the world (ip@hnrc.org);

- Reformation Heritage Books (RHB), a nonprofit organization that publishes two books per month, sells new (3,000 titles) and used books of Reformed and Puritan persuasion at discount rates, and provides free books to seminaries and pastors in Africa and to prisoners as enabled. Quarterly catalogs are available (RHB, 2965 Leonard N.E., Grand Rapids, Michigan 49525, 616-977-0599, orders@heritagebooks. org; on-line, www.heritagebooks.org). (Though the IP and RHB are, strictly speaking, independent from the denomination, most members of both boards are HRC members.)

Additionally, because the HRC considers reading literature from the Reformed heritage very important, many churches have their own bookstores and libraries. Finally, the denomination supports numerous non-denominational ministries, such as Trinitarian Bible Society, Word and Deed, the Wycliffe Society, and various local ministries that reach out to the poor and aged. The National-International Disaster Fund sends out substantial sums of money to people in various areas in the world hit hard by famine or natural disasters.

Chapter 9

Reformed and Reforming:
A Personal Invitation to You

The HRC is far from being a perfect denomination, but we pray that by grace we would remain faithful to the biblical, Reformed truth doctrinally, experientially, and practically. We trust that God's Word is faithfully proclaimed, the sacraments are faithfully administered, and Christian discipline is practiced among the churches as commanded by Christ. We trust the Lord has enabled us in some measure to carry the banner of truth delivered to us by our Reformed forefathers without surrendering to corrupt influences that are incessantly at work to destroy the only foundation of salvation (Jesus Christ and Him crucified) or to undermine the experiential knowledge of God's only way of salvation.

The Reformation church had a slogan: *ecclesia reformata semper reformanda*, which means the church must be Reformed and always reforming. The church must always strive to be closer to the principles and truths of Scripture in its doctrine and walk. We pray that we would be an ever-reforming church so that we may increasingly resemble "the Acts 2 church" of the New Testament, repenting, believing, growing, and continuing "steadfastly in the apostles' doctrine and fellowship, and in breaking of bread, and in prayers" (v. 42). Pray with us that we, as churches and as a denomination, will be faithful to this scriptural model and Reformation slogan.

Your Invitation

- If you are not attending church or are attending a church that is not true to Scripture, would you like to attend a church that is not afraid to proclaim all that the Bible teaches?
- Do you want to understand more fully and seriously live the teachings of the Scripture?
- Do you share the beliefs and vision contained in this booklet?

If so, please prayerfully consider attending a Heritage Reformed congregation and eventually joining our church family and church denomination as a professing member. We yearn to see you along with each of our members grow closer to the Lord—to be blessed and to be a blessing among us.

Please join us in our goal of growing in the grace and knowledge of Christ Jesus and of living to God's glory. Lend us your God-given gifts, talents, and service, and join us in our vision of spreading Reformed, Puritan, experiential preaching and teaching throughout local churches and around the world by every legitimate gospel means, looking to the Holy Spirit to add His blessing. Above all, pray with us that we would see days of great spiritual awakening and revival so that the earth will be filled with the knowledge of the Lord, from sea to sea.

Appendix 1

A Doctrinal Summary of the Six Major Divisions of Reformed Theology

Bartel Elshout

The Doctrine of God

The Bible is, in the first place, God's revelation of Himself and of His will. It reveals that the Creator of the universe, who is the primary Author of the Bible, is a Triune God and eternally exists in three Persons—the Father, the Son, and the Holy Spirit. These three Persons are one God, the same in substance, equal in power and glory (John 1:1; 2 Tim. 3:16-17; 1 John 5:7; 2 Cor. 13:14). It is especially in the Person of the Son, who is the Living Word of God (John 1:1), that the Father has revealed Himself to man (John 1:18; Heb. 1:1-3), and it is the explicit work of the Holy Spirit to glorify the Son (John 16:14).

The Doctrine of Man

The Bible provides us with God's view of man. It reveals to us that, at the beginning of time, God created man in the image of His eternal Son (Rom. 8:29), namely, with perfect knowledge, righteousness, and holiness. The chief purpose of man's creation and existence was to give glory to God with his entire being. Tragically, however, man rebelled against God and became a sinner, no longer answering the purpose for which he was created. Ever since man turned away from God, he is separated from God (spiritually dead), has a will entirely opposed to God, is the object of the wrath of God, and is unwilling and unable to be saved and restored to a right relationship with God (Gen. 1:27; Isa. 43:7b, 21; Eccl. 7:29; Rom. 8:7; 3:10, 11).

The Doctrine of Christ

The Bible reveals God's remedy to bring about reconciliation between an offended God and sinful man. He gave His only begotten and eternal Son, the Lord Jesus Christ. Being very God and very man, Jesus Christ possesses the perfect qualities to be the supreme Mediator between God and man. By His perfect obedience to the law of God as well as His total surrender to the punishment due to sin, He quenched the wrath of God and met all the requirements of God's justice by His death on Calvary's cross. As evidence of His Father's approval of His work as Mediator, Jesus arose from the dead and returned to the presence of His Father in heaven as the victorious and exalted Mediator. He has thereby fully opened the way for the relationship between God and man, broken by sin, to be completely restored (2 Cor. 5:17-21; 1 Tim. 2:5; Gal. 4:4-5; Rom. 5:1).

The Doctrine of Salvation

The Bible teaches that the will of sinful man is entirely opposed to God's will and that therefore man of his own volition will never seek reconciliation with God. That is why the work of the Holy Spirit is indispensable in the salvation of sinners. He alone can convince man of his sin and his need of Christ; He alone can cause man to surrender to God and work faith in Christ for salvation; He alone can preserve this salvation by dwelling in sinners. Since the salvation of sinners is the result of God's eternal initiative, God, by His Spirit, will effectively conquer the hearts of sinners and thus save His people from their sins (John 1:12, 13; 6:63a; 16:7-15; Gal. 1:15, 16a; Phil. 1:6; 2:13).

The Doctrine of the Church

The Bible teaches that the Holy Spirit, being a God of order, unites all those whom He saves into a body of believers called the church. It is within the context of the church that He causes His Word to be preached by men whom He has specifically called and qualified for this task. By means of the preaching of His Word, God is pleased to regenerate spiritually dead sinners and bestow upon them the gift of saving faith in the Lord Jesus Christ. He also uses the preaching of the Word to strengthen the faith of His people, causing them to grow in the grace and the knowledge of the Lord Jesus Christ. Thus the church is the place where God dwells in the midst of His people by means of His Word and Spirit. It is where His people worship God, receive spiritual nourishment from His Word, serve Him, and have fellowship with Him (Ps. 122; 132:13-18; Ps. 133; Acts 2:47; Heb. 10:24-25).

The Doctrine of the Last Things

The Bible teaches us that this age will come to an end and that the Lord Jesus Christ will return personally, visibly, and bodily to judge all mankind. Those who by God's grace believe in Him and have served Him will be ushered into His everlasting presence to rejoice in His glory with unspeakable joy. All who have rejected God's Son in unbelief and preferred a life of sin over the service of God, however, will be separated from God's favor forever in hell. There they will suffer unspeakable and eternal agony, being the object of God's just wrath upon sin (Matt. 25:31-46; Mark 13:26, 27; 2 Cor. 5:10; 2 Thess. 1:8-10; 2 Tim. 4:1, Rev. 20:11-12).

Appendix 2

A Personal Summary
of the Reformed Faith

Benjamin B. Warfield

1. I believe that my one aim in life and death should be to glorify God and enjoy Him forever; and that God teaches me how to glorify and enjoy Him in His holy Word, that is, the Bible, which He has given by the infallible inspiration of His Holy Spirit in order that I may certainly know what I am to believe concerning Him and what duty He requires of me.

2. I believe that God is a Spirit, infinite, eternal, and incomparable in all that He is; one God but three persons, the Father, Son, and the Holy Ghost, my Creator, my Redeemer, and my Sanctifier; in whose power and wisdom, righteousness, goodness, and truth I may safely put my trust.

3. I believe that the heavens and the earth, and all that in them is, are the work of God's hands; and that all He has made He directs and governs in all their actions; so that they fulfill the end for which they were created, and I who trust in Him shall not be put to shame but may rest securely in the protection of His almighty love.

4. I believe that God created man after His own image, in knowledge, righteousness, and holiness, and entered into a covenant of life with Him upon the sole condition of the obedience that was His due, so that it was by willfully sinning against God that man fell into the sin and misery in which I have been born.

5. I believe, that, being fallen in Adam, my first father, I am by nature a child of wrath, under the condemnation of God and corrupted in body and soul, prone to evil, and liable to eternal death; from which dreadful state I cannot be delivered save through the unmerited grace of God my Savior.

6. I believe that God has not left the world to perish in its sin, but out of the great love wherewith He has loved it, has from all eternity graciously chosen

unto Himself a multitude which no man can number, to deliver them out of
their sin and misery, and of them to build up again in the world His kingdom
of righteousness; in which [kingdom] I may be assured I have my part, if I
hold fast to Christ the Lord.

7. I believe that God has redeemed His people unto Himself through Jesus
Christ our Lord; who, though He was and ever continues to be the eternal
Son of God, yet was born of a woman, born under the law, that He might
redeem them that are under the law. I believe that He bore the penalty due
to my sins in His own body on the tree, and fulfilled in His own person the
obedience I owe to the righteousness of God, and now presents me to His
Father as His purchased possession, to the praise of the glory of His grace
forever; wherefore renouncing all merit of my own, I put all my trust only in
the blood and righteousness of Jesus Christ my Redeemer.

8. I believe that Jesus Christ my Redeemer, who died for my offenses was
raised again for my justification, and ascended into the heavens, where He
sits at the right hand of the Father Almighty, continually making intercession
for His people, and governing the whole world as head over all things for
His church: so that I need fear no evil and may surely know that nothing can
snatch me out of His hands and nothing can separate me from His love.

9. I believe that the redemption wrought by the Lord Jesus Christ is effectually
applied to all His people by the Holy Spirit, who works faith in me and
thereby unites me to Christ, renews me in the whole man after the image
of God, and enables me more and more to die unto sin and to live unto
righteousness; until, this gracious work having been completed in me, I shall
be received into glory; in which great hope abiding, I must ever strive to
perfect holiness in the fear of God.

10. I believe that God requires of me, under the gospel, first of all, that,
out of a true sense of my sin and misery and apprehension of His mercy
in Christ, I should turn with grief and hatred away from sin and receive and
rest upon Jesus Christ alone for salvation; that, so being united to Him, I may
receive pardon for my sins and be accepted as righteous in God's sight, only
for the righteousness of Christ imputed to me and received by faith alone:
and thus only do I believe I may be received into the number and have a right
to all the privileges of the sons of God.

11. I believe that, having been pardoned and accepted for Christ's sake, it is

further required of me that I walk in the Spirit whom He has purchased for me, and by whom love is shed abroad in my heart; fulfilling the obedience I owe to Christ my King; faithfully performing all the duties laid upon me by the holy law of God my heavenly Father; and ever reflecting in my life and conduct, the perfect example that has been set me by Christ Jesus my Leader, who died for me and granted to me His Holy Spirit so that I may do the good works which God has afore prepared that I should walk in them.

12. I believe that God has established His church in the world and endowed it with the ministry of the Word and the holy ordinances of Baptism, the Lord's Supper, and prayer; in order that through these means, the riches of His grace in the gospel may be made known to the world, and, by the blessing of Christ and the working of His Spirit in them that by faith receive them, the benefits of redemption may be communicated to His people; wherefore also it is required of me that I attend on these means of grace with diligence, preparation, and prayer, so that through them I may be instructed and strengthened in faith, and in holiness of life and in love; and that I use my best endeavors to carry this gospel and convey these means of grace to the whole world.

13. I believe that as Jesus Christ has once come in grace, so also is He to come a second time in glory, to judge the world in righteousness and assign to each His eternal award. I believe that if I die in Christ, my soul shall be at death made perfect in holiness and go home to the Lord; and when He shall return in His majesty, I shall be raised in glory and made perfectly blessed in the full enjoyment of God to all eternity. Encouraged by this blessed hope, it is required of me willingly to take my part in suffering hardship here as a good soldier of Christ Jesus, being assured that if I die with Him, I shall also live with Him; if I endure, I shall also reign with Him.

> And to Him, my Redeemer,
> with the Father,
> and the Holy Spirit,
> Three Persons, one God,
> be glory forever, world without end,
> Amen and Amen.

— *Selected Shorter Writings,* 1:407-410

The church's one foundation
Is Jesus Christ her Lord;
She is His new creation
By water and the Word;
From heaven He came and sought her
To be His holy bride;
With His own blood He bought her,
And for her life He died.

— Samuel John Stone